BOX POEMS

Willa Schneberg

OLD SHEETS

Larkin Warren

PS
589
S3

Box Poems   copyright © 1979 by Willa Schneberg
Old Sheets   copyright © 1979 by Larkin Warren

Library of Congress Catalogue Number 78-74231
ISBN 0-914086-25-1
Printed in the United States of America

Sculpture by Willa Schneberg
Cover and book design by Bruce Kennett and Willa Schneberg
Cover photograph by Stephen A. Sylvester
Photograph of Willa Schneberg by Edward Braverman
Photograph of Larkin Warren by Margot Page
Typeset by Jeffrey Schwartz
Paste-up by Allison Platt

Thanks to the editors of the following publications in which
versions of the poems from *Box Poems* appeared or will appear:
*The Village Voice, Gargoyle, Bitterroot, 100 Flowers Poetry
Anthology, Small Moon.*

Thanks for valuable assistance to Donna Gordon, Karen Propp,
Ellen Schon and Vera Hurwitz.

Some of the poems from *Old Sheets* have previously appeared in
*Aegis, Green House, The New Hampshire Times, Tendril, Small
Pond,* and *Quarterly West.*

The publication of this book was assisted by the Massachusetts
Council on the Arts and Humanities.

ALICE JAMES BOOKS   Printed at Tramp Printers
138 Mt. Auburn Street
Cambridge, Massachusetts 02138

91797

BOX POEMS

Table of Contents

OLD SHEETS

Table of Contents

BOX POEMS

Willa Schneberg

for Mark Weyne and my parents

ONE:
MY FIRST HOUSE

My first house was built —
four walls with a roof made of straw.
It had no floor.
Every holiday we
put sand on the floor and scraped it
with a shovel.
There was no electric. Inside the house,
was built out of brick, a big stove.
I slept on top of it. I had eight sisters.
I was the only brother.
The house had double windows.
We ate frozen apples.

Sam Smeed
Resident, Hebrew Rehabilitation Center for Aged

IMMIGRANT

I

Bubba came to America
on a ship so over-crowded
she had to stand in her own piss.
After she carried rich peoples'
children into bed,
she pored over their readers
wetting her thumb to turn the pages.

II

She was miserable
all those years
she couldn't work.
Her husband said,
*A man can't hold up his head
if his wife goes to business.*

After her husband, the milkman
with no business-head died,
she bought the corset store.
She fit any woman
whether she smelled
or was missing two breasts.
Every day she went to the bank.

III

But Bubba couldn't dispose of her
son-in-law's illness
like an empty box —
its brassieres sold.
How could she understand him?
A college boy, American born
with a wife and daughter,
walking out of his classroom,
forgetting his students' names
and why he was teaching.

IV

Bubba visited him in the hospital
and brought him pajamas.
On the pocket
she embroidered his initials.

He flicked cigarette ashes
in his lap.
She was sure
she could snap him out of it.
His face between her hands
she screamed at him,
Be a man!

BONES

After the morning shock treatment
he was tossed on the black chair
crumpled and flat
a shirt without a chest.

His wife piled the bones neatly
on the upholstered arm.
His daughter played with the bones,
arranged them into a skeleton
and was angry when he wouldn't wear it.

Now that she is older
she understands.
Often her body cannot support her bones.
They slip out looking for a grave.

FAMILY

He drove the car
like a knife
he was going to stick
in someone's ribs.
On those long rides
in the country
I sat between them,
my mother and I
discussing his silence.

PICKLING

She dreamt he was sliced
up in a jar
like the artichokes and tomatoes
he so loved to pickle.
But there he was
at the refrigerator as usual —
shoving artichokes and
tomatoes into jars,
controlling what he could.

THE SEPARATION

My father left us only once,
when I was seven.
For six months
he lived in Aunt Sophie's
finished basement.
It had orange ashtrays
that matched the toilet seat.
I visited him and
watched the baby guppies
in the fish tank
being eaten by their fathers.

My mother seemed more relaxed
than usual, but she sat even longer
in the bathroom reading.
I loved the quiet.

After my father took me
on a trip to the wine country
of upstate New York,
he moved back with us.
Nothing was different,
except he didn't leave again.

THAT NIGHT

In my apartment
we expose our porcupine fish,
bloated and spiny.
Plopping them one by one
on the table,
we watch them squirm.

You aren't the uncle
who told me I could do anything.
I'm not the niece entranced
by your linguistic acrobatics
while you reign
in your wheelchair
at weddings and bar mitzvahs.

I tell you I practiced
being paralyzed.
When I was seven,
I cradled one leg like a baby and lowered it gently
on the other one above the knee.
At twenty-one I wake up
to go back to sleep.
You tell me, *Now we both know
how to be crippled.*

Lie with me.
We'll flatten out
like porcupine fish.
If you say no,
I'll settle for a cup of tea.

I imagine the rope
hanging over your bed,
the rope you grip
to move on to Faye and
ask you to tell me about Luxembourg
when you were stationed there
in the war.

TRILOGY

THE SON

My mother lies
about little things.
She's been coloring her
gray for years.
I found bottles in her bathroom.
She tells everybody
her sister is the older one.
I ask for Coke.
She says I drank it up.
I find a carton
in the vegetable bin.

She lies about promises too.
She swore she wouldn't tell anyone
I flunked three subjects,
but she told Aunt Sarah,
If he had as much curiosity
about history as he does
about Houdini's escapes,
he'd be a straight A student.

I told her to drop dead,
that she never loved me
from the minute I started getting fat
and she couldn't show me off
to company anymore.

I love my father.
He has more guts than
all the men who can walk put together.
He treats me like an adult.
He says, *How can you expect*
your mother to give to you
when she wants to be the child?

THE MOTHER

Fresh from my bath
wearing my silk robe
my hair free
I walk Kippers in the back yard.
The tomatoes are still green,
the bird house empty.

While Kenny watches T.V.
and stuffs his face with pretzels,
I make silver jewelry —
bracelets with delicate bands,
pinky rings with opals.
The teachers at school
want to pay me more than I charge.

I come home exhausted
and make a roast
with potatoes and broccoli.
I set the table —
put out mustard and ketchup.
Kenny decides he wants MacDonald's.
You little bastard, I scream
if you leave this house,
I'll never cook you another meal,
so help me God!

His father who hopes
that with the next Big Mac
everything will be fine,
chauffeurs his son.

Maybe they won't return this time.
Then I'll pick apples and pears
put them in
a Ming bowl
till they're soft enough to eat.

THE FATHER

Polio knocked me down
four months before Salk
invented the vaccine.

Faye practically lived in the hospital.
She'd pick a word out of the dictionary.
The game was to guess the meaning.
The doctors would contradict themselves:
I would not have long to live,
I would be a quadriplegic,
I would regain full use of my limbs.
I told her to take the dictionary home.

I left a year later
not the Harvard Law grad to be the first Jewish president—
but a paraplegic.
Faye had to learn
to wheel me over curbs
and be the man in bed.

My wife who wore shoes
with a bag to match,
let dirt build up underneath her nails
and didn't change her dress.

After we thought we couldn't have children
Kenny was born.
Once he hid all her stones,
topaz and turquoise,
lapis lazuli and moonstones,
hoping she'd fondle him
the way she did them.

But Kenny will leave this house,
lose weight and find
other women to love him.

TWO:
ALL ALONE

All alone on a Friday night.
Garlic and onion on my breath.
Who's to know.

Martin Reiss
Member, Psychiatric Evening Program
Post-Graduate Center for Mental Health

SUCCA

She felt like a candle
surrounded by chandeliers,
but very happy.
The girls everyone wanted
to sit next to,
who kiss boys alone in rooms
had finally invited her
to the playground after school.

It was necessary to spin
a hula hoop for five minutes.
She began swinging her hips
but almost immediately
the hoop dropped.
The leader, the girl who had gone
almost all the way, taunted,
cracking her gum,
You're not cool enough
to come to our parties.

She ran straight
to the succa over the garage.
The ladder carried her inside.
The lulovs and ferns
tacked to the plywood walls,
the green peppers and garlic
dangling from the beams,
the bowls swelling with dates,
figs, etrogs, cranshaw melons,
honeydews told her—
Don't need those girls.

She held a Spanish onion
in her palm,
a crackly plum coat
hid the moon-like body.
The covering slid off easily
like her nightgown before a shower.
She stripped off thin layers and
let herself cry.

ELEGY

We saw each other in the Village
a few years ago.
His Jewish afro was blue.
We walked to the Trucks
parked near the Morton Street Pier.
Men were zipping their flies,
buttoning their jackets.

I told him I don't sleep with
strangers anymore, only friends.
He said, *There are only strangers.*
In the trucks at night
I don't listen to
involvement's whines,
only pleasure's ahs.

We were twelve when we met.
His veins bulged in his skinny arms.
I told him he would make a perfect junkie.

I found a birthday card he made me,
in a shoebox with old letters.
I see him sitting in the dinette
of his mother's house in the project
cutting up National Geographic, Mad,
Ladies Home Journal
searching for turtles, dinosaurs, babies,
Brillo pads, geraniums and monsters
to glue on the cover with Elmer's.
Underneath, he wrote,
All my friends wish you...
and inside was his picture
taken in a photo booth
in the 14th Street subway,
his tongue sticking out,
... and I, myself, wish you
a very happy birthday.

FRIENDS

for Nancy

Two women in a canoe
paddle with their hands.
The canoe ties to a low branch.
Lines in their palms peel off
to trails that blaze through woods.
Deer come out of hiding
and wait on the bank.
The friends perch in treetops —
two clouds
peering through each other,
they guard their roads.

GIGANTIC ROOM

There must be a gigantic room
where in a place of honor
a simple vase holds
a day lily,
and the pterodactyl, mesophippus,
mastodon, australopithecine,
awk, passenger pigeon,
chatterton, plath
sit on mats holding cups
warm with tea
between their paws, claws, hooves, hands.

ONE NIGHT STAND A L'HOTEL L'ETOILE

In Joseph Cornell's box
there are no disappointments.
I come to this box when Cornell isn't
waltzing with Cerrito or Grisi
He and I know that only here
they are sisters of Beatrice.
In the street they might answer
him with four-letter words.
I unstrap my satin toe shoes
gently place the voile, the black beads,
the dry flowers in the corner.
And wait for the stranger who will
kiss me all over and let me come first.

His lips rush across my body like an ocean,
burying conch shells and pearls in my pores.

MACKEREL

In the kitchen he tears up bread
mixing it with mackerel and milk.
I sit.
He waits as the male cat pulls
out of the female.
Then whistles to them softly.
Still smelling from fish,
he goes into the other room with me.
I arch my back on the bed.

MEMORY OF A FULL MOON

I

The fisherman's wife
unfolds a spotless housedress
for Willa to slip on.
She offers Robert
her husband's flannel robe,
a pipe with a clay bowl
forgotten in the torn pocket.
She wraps their drenched clothes
around the curve of the pot-bellied stove.

II

The fisherman announces,
The man who wears the robe
smokes the pipe!
His wife brings out bottles
of Old Schooner's Ale.
I fear for the ship that hasn't
made it back to shore.
When a storm rages up on a full moon,
she'll go down sure as I've shot
a harpoon into a whale's side.
The fisherman plays harmonica
to the Irish tune
BIBBING MY CAP BEHIND ME.
The women dance the jig,
their arms about each other's shoulders.

III

I awaken
in the middle of the night
in the frail wooden house.
Sitting on the rocker
I watch Robert sleep.
The smell of dried fish
clings to my fingers.
I rock and think
this night will be
the past soon.

IV

The rain is faint
in the morning.
The fisherman's wife smooths
the patchwork quilt covering them
and whispers in Willa's ear
A woman who sleeps on her left side
will have many lovers but no husband.
Robert's arm around Willa's waist,
the two lie on their left side —
removed from the future
as drowning sailors.

WHY I DON'T WANT TO BE A BANYAN TREE

I thought I wanted to be you —
a forest all by myself,
like one hundred Shivas
becoming all arms, swinging
until they rest on soil
my fingers above ground,
not hidden like dead things.

Banyan tree,
I don't want to be you.
You can't wonder.
It's I who gives you magic.
You can't marvel how thin light
snuggles in your thousand curves.

THE FURNITURE

I left him over the furniture.

According to him
the drapes are all right,
the sofa not bad, the lampshade nice,
the rugs will do.

To me the summer drapes
have a fishnet look.
You have to stop making supper
to watch the sunset squeeze through.

The sofa was made in the thirties
to look Victorian.
The back is heart shaped.
The wine colored brocade
faded like graduation flowers
I saved in a book.
A person can stretch out and sleep
good as in his own bed.

The tin lampshade has bells
cut into it around the middle.
They don't ring but the light
that leaks out is perfect
for late night reading.

The rug quite frankly hurts the eyes.
It was made from horse rein
and spiralled into an oval.
When I was a kid,
I wrapped whatever wool
I found in the house
around the nails and yanked.
Look straight into it.
Doesn't it have the shape of a cyclone?

It was all fair and square.
I took the color
and left him the outlines.

METAMORPHOSIS OF A FROG

for Maria Sibylla Merian (1647-1717)

She left specimens behind —
preserved spiders, pickled worms,
dead as her marriage.
In Surinam,
she would only draw moths
that alight on the shoulder.

On parchment using watercolors
she meticulously
revealed the structure
of a leaf, a wing.

She walked amongst the natives,
in her arms enough bananas,
papayas, pomegranates
for a week of drawing,
a week of eating.
The natives made her reed bowls,
gave recipes for breadfruit.

She observed the lifecycle
of butterflies so bright they made
stained glass seem pale,
when most people believed insects emerged
fully formed from garbage.

PRINT SHOP FRIDAY AFTERNOON

"e"s distributed in their large spaces,
double "f"s in their tiny spaces,
chases upright in the rack,
joints squirted with oil.
When the old men leave
the metal plates gleam.

All week talk's hard above
the presses wheeze.
Rollers slide against type,
beds follow — their paper
poised for impression.

Friday afternoon
no hands jerk the handles
clanking the machines into motion.
No one is there to name this
upside-down mirror writing:
language.

IN MY SHOPPE

I don't let in no men or kids.
Agnes, all 300 lbs. of her,
a Thinny-Thin Shake in one hand,
a Baby Ruth in the other,
sits next to me.
Her Infant of Prague for over the T.V.
is still warm from the kiln.
She moves it back and forth
next to her crotch
until I crack a smile.
The girls come here to get away.
They leave the supper on the stove
and let their husbands pull
the kids off each other.
Selma gums a decal on a
heart box for her honey.
I tell her don't put decals
all over it or it will look cheap.
Barbara smoothes the mold line
on the Nubian slave girl.
I say for the right brown,
three coats of stain
rubbed in real good.

The girls know this is my shop.
They do as I do
and don't ask questions.
I never got no trouble
until this Jewish girl
who went to college for ceramics
started noseying around.
She claims she fashions shapes
on the potter's wheel,
makes glazes from powders.
I can read their minds like a book.
She wants to pick my brains
for next to nothing,
then open her own shop.
I told her
we don't want no artists.

THREE:
I SIT

I sit in the sitting room-dining room
next to the window.
Then I smoke
    with my circle.
    Things begin to happen.
        When I keep my circle going
            everything is peachy.

Mary King
Resident, Provident Nursing Home

A PIECE OF THE CAKE

Fred, it cost me a bundle
but I got my money's worth.
You know the place
down by the new development —
the Mafia joint
called *Wind in the Willows.*

They keep the bar open
after serving the wedding cake.
And let me tell you —
when I wanted a shot of Chivas,
I just went behind the bar
and helped myself.

I didn't have a fancy wedding.
To tell you the truth,
my wife's father was dead.
He couldn't hold a job,
left them nothing except bills.
We said our *I do's*
on her mother's screened-in porch.
My mother made a chocolate cake.
We got a $25 bond, a mix-master
and a knife set.

I was going overseas,
scared to death I'd be knocked off
before I did anything except press clothes
in Weir's Laundry after school.
At least I would be a married man.
Abby was a good girl —
wouldn't go all the way
until we married.

My daughter was giving it away for free.
Now he'll have to pay
the $30,000 mortgage on the Hanley Place.

We were the first
in the wedding party procession.
They announced *Mr. and Mrs. Paulson.*
We walked slow as a bath
on Sunday morning.
I will never forget the applause.
It felt better than when
I got the promotion.

35

PORNO MOVIE WATCHER

The row is empty.
I sink low in my seat
and open my fly.

I wonder what the girl with
the butterfly tattoo
on the inside of her thigh
does off screen.
Maybe she lives in a trailer
and travels around.
I could make her stay in one place!
I'd put large cinder blocks underneath
the trailer's chassis,
add on an aluminum porch.

I'd introduce her to Bill
my only friend—
if I knew where he was.
He couldn't make a chick either.

We had good times
sitting around in the afternoon,
drinking beer,
girlie magazines strewn all over the floor,
seeing whose come shot out farther.

FORCED VACATION

I eat unrecognizable food
through a tube in my nose.
John calls three times a day.
He says I shouldn't get any skinnier
or he'll have nothing to squeeze.
I can feel every bone in my body
as if there was no skin covering them,
but I know I have never looked so good.
John will soon see me through my eyes.
Gloria from Flying Fish, called to say,
We'll twirl the batons extra hard for you.
The girls from Arista phoned,
I've been elected again.
Mrs. Allen wrote me,
Don't worry about homework.
You'll make it up.

I look out the window.
It has snowed.
When the sun's strong
snow flashes diamonds.
I never paid much attention to it before.
It was just there for me to ski on.
It's nice not to have to do anything.

WHALER WIFE'S LAMENT

He wrote from Zanzibar,
I eat salt junk tough
as an old shoe,
but pretend I'm eating
your cranberry pie,
the crust light as my head
after the last bible leaf is tried.
I'm scrimshawing you a jagging wheel,
its body a sea serpent,
its head a unicorn's
with a fork for the horn.
It will crimp your crusts,
prick holes for steam.

After four years of chasing whales—
he comes home again,
his clothes stinking of oil.
The first month is always good.
We sit after supper.
He holds his hands out.
I wind yarn around them.

He tells me about people
in the Sandwich Islands
who don't know winter
or a Christian God
and about the sick whale he was
sure had a belly-full of ambergris.
He poked inside her
for the treasure that makes perfume
even captains' wives can't afford.
His crewmates stood silent waiting
for nothing.

Too soon for arguing
about the little money
he brings home,
after he pays for his clothes
from the slop chest
and the whiskey he swills
down like water.
I bite my lip and bear it
like I do the years
without him.

He'll ship out the day after Easter
now that he's eaten so much cranberry
that he has the runs
and has made me pregnant
with another child who
I'll tell stories of his father
single-handedly harpooning
a sperm whale
big as an iceberg.

SELF-ABUSE VICTIM, FERNALD SCHOOL

Alone in the shower stall
she bangs her head against tile
until she bleeds.
She watches fascinated
as the water swirls
the blood she made herself
down the drain.

Soon the nurse
will give her aluminum foil,
knowing she likes the sound
when she crumples it,
and will hold her head
and dress her wound.

A HOUSEWIFE'S REVENGE

Home was safe.
She couldn't be hurt
in rooms she gave life to.
There wasn't a design on a plate
she hadn't agonized over.
Each object where she placed it —
the magazine rack
next to the occasional chair,
the flat-bowled wooden spoon
over the stove.

Every morning since she stayed inside
she took out different utensils,
fondling them like gifts from a lover.
She turned the eggbeaters crank
to see the whiz of air.
She traced her finger along
the corkscrew's spiral as if
it were a turreted shell.

Her husband never mentioned it,
but when he handled
the garlic press or even the soap dish,
they felt weightless.

VAMPIRES

for Miracle Mitchell

She is too fat to sit
in the bathtub so we soap her standing up.
She likes the way soap
and water licks her legs,
thick and tough as elephant hide
and disappears in the folds
of her mashed potato flesh.

This is her 11th mental hospital
but she moved to her own world
almost full-time years ago.

Whistling between her teeth,
swaying from side to side
in the tub
she talks vampires.
They steal the mirrors of good women
and give them new ones —
black-eyed babies who will
grow up to sell strawberries and peaches
even in the winter time.
Vampires attack the jugular of bad people
decapitate them and carry their hideous faces
on poles through towns and villages,
warning other evil ones.

We don't bother to check
the doors and windows.
Knowing she has already escaped,
we help her over the side of the bath
and wrap her in two large towels.

TRIP TO NAHANT BEACH
AFTER FIVE YEARS INSIDE

Before my accident I worked as a lumper
hauling freight on and off ships.
I don't know about the other guys.
In my dreams I have two legs.
Can you believe it?
I can't find a single shoe vendor
to sell me one shoe.

Me and the other legless wonders
wheel ourselves along the path
above the sunbathers.
I don't know what's more wonderful,
the sea breeze on my face,
the fresh smell of the ocean,
the sound of the waves crashing
or the half-naked girls.
I have my eye on one in particular.
Her bathing suit top ties around her neck.
The sun dries the beads of wet on her legs.
A boy shares the blanket with her.
She cuts peaches into sections,
feeds them to him,
then saves the pits in a plastic bag.

I save things too —
bargain coupons for Snow's Clam Chowder
and Purina Dog Chow,
playing cards from odd decks,
and flashlight batteries,
a little life left
in them yet.

KAHAN AT HOME

One corner of the red oilcloth,
on a table in the activities room,
intrigues him.
He pushes it open and closed
with his thumb.
He tries to fold it neatly
as he had his wife's Shabbos napkins,
but it falls in a heap.

His wife lives one floor below
In the elevator he tells me,
I am a Kahan.
When my roommate is asleep,
I try to make the sign
of my chosen class of a chosen people,
but my hands won't listen. See!
He can't place his pinky next to his ring finger,
his middle finger next to his index finger.
I'm forbidden to attend funerals.
They won't let me lay a stone
on my wife's grave.
It's written that I can only remarry
a pure one —
a girl who has bedded with none
but her mother.

We walk towards a woman
violently rocking in a wheelchair,
her catheter full.
He says, *Listen for*
the rain on the tin roof.
My mother is waiting.
I have to let it plop
in a small cup.

See your wife first, Mr. Horowitz.
He presses his lips against the cheek
of the woman I bring him to.
He whispers, *I had a wife*
I couldn't fondle
when the sheets were blood-stained.

A HISTORY

She leaves the nursing home
without telling anyone she is going.
She has nothing to do with
the other old women,
discarded by their children too,
who spend their days waiting
from one meal to the next.

Her place is the third chair in
at the long oak table
of Boston Public Library's Reserve Room
where she and her husband spent many evenings,
she reading Janson's HISTORY OF ART,
he reading Will and Ariel Durants'
volumes of civilization.
Before completing the AGE OF NAPOLEON, Volume IV
he died.

Excited as a child waiting for her mother
to whisk sweet cream into whipped,
she opens her spiral notebook
uncaps her ball point pen.

Courbet's SELF PORTRAIT WITH BLACK DOG
shares a page with Millet's THE SOWER.
She thinks of her parents
leaving the wheat fields at sunset in Radomysl.
Weary of making someone else rich,
creeping back to their cottage
to wash themselves in the large tin tub
before preparing supper
of pumpernickel and thick soup
for the children.

When she finds herself in a corridor,
its door locking behind her,
she doesn't call out.
She waits,
listening for the voices of her family
already history.

OLD SHEETS

Larkin Warren

for my grandmothers,
who fill my house,
for their children,
and for Dennis

I

AT THE WINDOW

One hip
hard against the cold
prodding counter edge
she stands
snapping new green beans

tossing them headless
into the yellow bowl
for washing.

Beyond the window
the field moves
silently
to the bottom of the sky.

Her hands stop

then begin again,
breaking the stillness,
bean-ends
like knuckles snapping
in her kitchen.

KANSAS MEDICINE SHOW, 1928

On the morning you are found missing
your mother says
It must be gypsies! Then she cries.

The neighbors know
you are the little girl who dances.
This constant tapping, these
dusty pirouettes, this insistence
on tulle, it drives everyone crazy.

Downtown, a man is singing cures,
amber syrups, mint powders.
On the back of his wooden truck,
you dance, tapping
in your mother's shoes, pretending
you don't know your audience.

That night, your mother trades tears
with you, takes away five silver dimes,
bites them, puts them in a jar.

The jar goes high on a shelf.
Later, you sneak it down, risking
a fall, discovery.
It's empty.

These days, dancers are everywhere.
These days, there is wordless singing
in your kitchen. Under the table,
your feet, tapping, insisting.

RUTH IN THE DUST BOWL

Harry, she says, don't forget
the bed.

But the truck is overloaded.
They will sleep on the ground,
he says, and the children
will make do with old quilts.
The bed stays in Oklahoma.
There were never any books.

The pots go to California, cookfire
by cookfire. One hundred ways
to boil potatoes.

Behind them, voices collect
in the old house,
small nameless insects.

Ruth leans, the sun rising
at her back, the sun setting
in her face.
Harry, she whispers at night,
Harry I'm afraid, maybe
I'm dying.

Harry sleeps, dreaming
No. 4, small juice, two
muffins, coffee.
The children, drymouthed,
dream of oranges.

RITUAL

For them, it begins at the grove of small,
damaged trees beside the highway.
The smell of flame and rubber
hangs in the air like trumpets.
Hands buried in their pockets, they walk
around, around, mumbling incantations.
They shade their eyes, they wonder
how fast? What time? Trees
are the only evidence.

Then the junkyard. In the silence
the car rests, a picked carcass
on the back of the truck bed.
There are first rites. The
car is touched. They kick at the dust,
sharing low sounds of disbelief.
Well, someone says, well.

Awkward in new clothes, they walk
up to the tin door of the trailer.
A woman opens the door. Past her
they see the quiet father, hunched over
in a chair.
Nothing is as real
as the yellow car, the absence of sound
in the junkyard.

MISERY LOVES

for B. and B.

You want to bury your dead,
but company is coming.

You open the door. They stand
before you
like carolers.
Their chorus, their litany of names
begins:
grandmother
cousin
wife
lover
child
brother
sister
father.

You carry their list with you,
names piled like coal
in a wooden cart.

You climb into your grief with them,
you are like a miner,
a light on your forehead.
Someone in front holds a canary
to tell you
when you have gone too far.

BARBARA'S HAIR

These knots are always appearing.
I comb my hair each morning,
strand by strand and now,
in mid-day, these knots are here,
knots tying themselves.

If I undo the knots, one by one,
everything is solved.
If I leave them
scattered like clover,
the night goes sour.
Wrong numbers call,
my lover is indifferent.
The kettle boils dry.
And no tea, no lamplight, feathers
go flying from the quilt.

LOVE POEM

A man and a woman are to be
sitting at table talking. Or
shall they remain silent.
            Virginia Woolf, *A Writer's Diary*

With the prong of your fork
you dig lines into the linen.
Patterns on the blue cloth deepen,
then disappear, like bruises.

I ask you why there are wings beating
outside the night window, why
the sparrow flew down the chimney
into the early September fire.
And that noise, instant screeching,
did we hear that?

You go on defining small spaces
with that fork, you go on.
That small burning bird, that screech,
did we hear that?

SUNDAY

Only people in the movies
take the phone off the hook.
Yet there it is,
smothered
with a striped pillow.
It has ceased to struggle.

Sunday meant Mass.
White gloves. A hat.
Daddy would take me.

Veins in a leaf
small ridges
faintly mapped on your skin
where your clothes had been.

Watching your eyes
I trace the belt line
of your waist,
follow it
with my fingers
from front to back

Where the line becomes
your spine,
a right angle to my touch,
unyielding.

Lust and the Times
in a bed as wide
as summer. Silence
washes over us
like amazing grace.

IRRECONCILABLE DIFFERENCES

One of the symptoms is hair. Curl it,
cut it, color it another color, twist
it around your finger, remember
what it was to be the ugly child
at a birthday party.

Another sign is fingernails,
some kind of change in fingernails.
They are red as if by magic,
or geranium pink,
they no longer seem attached.
They flutter around your mouth
like bees.

And sleep. There is no pattern
to sleeping. It comes in waves,
rolling you back to bed
in the morning, or thundering at you,
knotted up, wide awake at midnight
in a silent house.

About this house. It is the cleanest
on the block, or the dirtiest.
Children live here. You never see them,
but you know they live here.
They wet their beds, torture the cat,
have nightmares.

SLEEPING DOGS

You may not believe this.
I stayed as long as I could
the night you looked
deep into my eyes and calmly
pressed your thumb
into the soft butter
of my throat.
I thought to myself, Oh,
no.

Still.
I knew all along what was happening.
There was someone else like you.
One night I threw
the alarm clock.
It shattered on the wall
just above his head,
watch works flying, springs
and screws and glass
tearing small holes
in the flowered paper.

AFTERMATH

The cup of morning coffee still sits
beside the bed.
The coffee sits, cream gathered
like algae on a mountain pond.
I am alone here, and somewhere
you are sleeping in another bed
of unknown dimensions and
uncertain population.

This bed, however,
has a known periphery.
Like north country farmers
we have paced its boundaries
noting open spaces,
old stone markers. Too long,
wide and empty, it throws a shadow
that spreads to the doorway.

HOTHOUSE

I wonder
how the potted plants feel
about all this rain.

As they hang by the window
on silken cords,
do they hear music
of seasons changing
do they hear the rain
sliding down glass
a stain of blue light.

I fill the yellow pitcher
and give every one
a drink. I do it
nonchalantly.
It's not likely
they'll run away.

Do they conspire
among themselves?
I am a captor
of green things, I'll play

Ain't Nobody's Business
louder than the rain.

THE GARDENER

for Dan Field

He sits in the kitchen chair,
dying in Grandmother's quilt,
wrapped
in braid-trimmed red flannel.
He calls his children.
He calls his children, he
sends them away.
He parcels them out
like shoots from the grape arbor.

Once
he chased
his Indian-eyed wife
around the table
with a bread knife.

He looked like Gary Cooper,
she told him, later.

GRIEF

Like a drunk, it lurches
through the early morning
chased by dogs.

The flash bulb goes off
while your eyes are wide open.
The blue light burns
for days, just out of sight.
In the picture,
you look surprised.

A refrain like chained tires
clanking like a cripple
over frost heaves,
one link broken.

Water runs somewhere,
pipes humming in the wall.
In another room
a child talks in his sleep.

In a crowd, a man
steps down on your heel
and walks on.

DRIVING NORTH

The news of your death
hasn't yet reached the bars
and restaurants on Route 128.
Everything goes on as usual
here, people passing
on double yellows, rolling
through stops and reds.

I stop to buy a bottle of wine,
some cigarettes. Outside the car
heat leans on my shoulders
like damp hands at a funeral.

When I reach the mountains
the air changes, becomes cooler
and blue. The news must be out,
everyone is driving slowly.

I am moving closer to where
you are not.
From one side of your house
to another, whose heels hammer
the floor, advertising anger
to the silence downstairs?

TO THE GNOME WITH WHOM I LIVE

You are too old, my baby.
Old eyes at seven, my eyes in your face.
Glow worm child
beacon for my dark days,
summer in these mountains
where summer is too short.
You steal me, laughing.
Long slat of a boy, dreaming,
molding my dreams to fit your pockets.
Your sleep invades my peace.

This birth pull never stops, we are bound
together, pulling apart.
When you walk to the woods,
you've grown taller since Tuesday,
inches of skin flashing above your shoes,
pants too short.

You shine, I trust you.
Then you become lightning,
thunder and bitter rain, fierce
and fighting — whose eyes flash
back at me?
A sudden mountain storm.
I am left cold and wet,
damning you and motherhood.

MILL POND

for L. F.

1. In the clear morning, the man
and the small boy skate.
They test the ice like space men
on a new moon, carefully etching
figures, watching the shore
slide away.

Scratched circles and eights
grow wider, then are abandoned
for speed, for distance, down
the solid river, Durham to
Newmarket. Far below them
fish move in lazy circles.

2. The child no longer cares
about his fingers. His skates
come off hard, pulled like cork
from a bottle.

The man carries him to the car
like a sack of loose highway salt.
Daddy, the child breathes, the word
condenses in the air above them, almost
freezes. Daddy, daddy, he dreams,
knowing the rough smell of the man's neck.

At home, the unset fire.
Behind them, the pond, the fish,
the evening beginning.

HOSTAGES

If we do not watch the clock, it will be
time to play with grandchildren.

If we look carefully at our thumbs.

If we close our eyes.

If we remember all the words to some song.

If we remember: prayers.

If we lean carefully against this wall,
it will stay up.

II

OLD SHEETS

Sleeping alone
is best done in them.
Faded, limp
from too many washings
and history, they are
blue-flowered soft,
yielding without a fight
to dream thrashing,
tangling around shoulders
without being threatening.

Waking alone
is best done in them.
Familiar, scented
like the hollow
of an old lover's neck,
they are silent and knowing.
The stripes have no edges,
no anger,
gentle, like stuffed brown bears
of childhood.

BIRTHDAY PROMISE

for Jean

Hands pressed
on a cold white wall.

No blood welling on those same ivory
wrist bones, like roses on snow,
no rivers calling like old lovers,
no gas drawing me in like incense,
no pills for travelling,
no sliding into that sleep.

None of that.

A pen mysteriously inkless,
a typewriter with a sticking c key,
a child wanting always to be born,
a paper blank as insomnia—these
will not send me over.

I tell myself
clutter would be worse
than this isolation,
celibacy easier to manage
than a cast of thousands.

There is a thin gold chain
around my neck, a reminder
of the fragile difference
between raging
and a whine.

NIGHT PASSAGE

Only one subway token.
Open doors or other, larger
doors, closing.

Lines of docile people
winding through cattle fences,
people wanting the airport,
closed now, inaccessible.

Cab strike, garbage
and in the alley, someone
sings, glass shatters.

Who's singing?
Who knows? she
asks, waking up.

ONLY MOTHER OF AN ONLY CHILD

That grey car almost hit you.
I saw him skid, I watched
from the upstairs window.
He slipped, tires yelping,
fishtailed around you
and you
on that yellow bike,
you looked up,
untouched,
untouchable.

It made me angry.
I could have hit out
with a closed fist.

Every day you go
through the world
on your bike,
on the school bus,
with God only knows who driving,
who drives that bus,
anyway?

I watch the square of your back
as you ride away alone,
red jacket like a flag,
flying smaller and smaller,
disappearing.

FEVER, DECEMBER

The heat taps up into the pipes
like the cane of a blind man,
which way, which way. Outside,
the wind pushes trees
into icy submission.

I wake in a green, undersea light,
resenting something. The wind?
The blind man?
Numbers on the digital clock
glow, frozen, locked
at one-one-one.

My birthday is three days
before Christ is born
again, nine days before the year,
like a light, goes out.
My cracked lips
make me remember this.

Unknowing people burn candles for me,
ring bells, lift their glasses.
The small clacking of ice cubes,
the din of hymns, the weight
of my feet, asleep somewhere
at the bottom of this bed,
all these things
are part of our celebration.

UNEXPECTED VISITOR

A fanfare at the door.
Amazing
to open it and see you
grinning, leaning out of the wind
bringing some of my old years
in with you, like a parade.

Stomping the snow from your boots
you sit. We are knee to knee.
Inside me
there is a small joy burning
memories like logs stacked in the woodshed.

Beads on the abacus
balancing everything.
Like bears hearing music
we dance
on the ends of our sentences.

A flying visit and gone again.
You are my favorite trapeze artist.
Swoop in anytime.
And thanks,
I needed a small circus
in January.

SNOW

for T.O.

This storm finally blows in,
confirming our worst suspicions.
Alone, I set out
to clean things up.

The stoop first, then the sidewalk,
and moving slowly out into the road,
past the row of mailboxes, sentinels
full of assent, or denial.
Only one is mine
but I check them all
just to be sure.

Another two or three inches fall
filling the hollows behind me.
Again and again
I thrust with this shovel,
chunk, chunk
against snow-covered rock.

I work a path towards town,
wondering why no one else
is working. Are they sleeping?
Don't they want to dig out?

Hours later, in the odd light
of snowbanks, I shovel a trail home.
Tomorrow, I will set out again,
to break new blisters,
to clean things up.

PIG

That spring
Tibbetts' pig thought it was a dog.
Square to the ground, muddy-pink
and blossom-tailed, it would run
with the neighborhood mutts
through the fields,
through the garden,
breaking new corn stalks,
pulling laundry from lines.

The children would chase Tibbett' pig,
who was chasing the dogs.
Shrieking, oinking and barking,
the pack of them,
two-legged, four-legged,
they ran until slaughter season,
when they separated the pig
from the dogs.

It was very quiet.
The women and girls
fried ham
and took the laundry down.

TRYING TO TURN

To love a child is to turn
away from the patient dead,
who understand.
    William Matthews

You sing yourself to sleep and now
you dream your singing. Outside
there is a storm, trees cracking,
rain hitting the windows.
I sleep like oil on water,
your voice running beneath me,
rising when the wind does.

You wander in, a prophet
bringing your dream, weeping Yes,
Yes. I take you back to bed,
watch small bones shift in your face
as it folds back in to sleep.

Child, we are held here
like hostages, solitary as stone.
We will always dream our other lives,
we are every besieged and lonely thing,
insisting on Yes, Yes.

CALL FROM CRESTED BUTTE

I pick up the receiver and hear
your voice, fighting the din
of what you tell me is a pool hall.
Your father's laughter joins with yours.

Through an open window, I feel the snap
of early New England autumn.
When we have finished the see-yous
and love-yous,

I put the phone down, knowing
you have inherited this habit—
do something crazy, call me, tell me
all about it
always from too many miles away.

MAKING THINGS UP

Every journey into the past
is complicated by delusions,
false memories, false naming
of real events.
      Adrienne Rich, *Of Woman Born*

1.

You arrive on time, singing, glad
to be here. I take all these roses,
put them someplace appropriate.
This vase? The middle of the bed?

2.

Delighted when the child is born,
you parade him through the streets
like a small purple banner.

3.

On all our picnics, ants bring daisies,
forming one of those chains.
They never walk across our blanket,
never walk through the potato salad.

We are reassured by these rituals.

4.

Ripe old age. Retrospective
exhibits. Every symphony
very finished.
No one dies early.

DREAM POEM

You call at midnight.
You get me out of the bathtub,
dripping and shivering,
book in hand.

That moat, you say,
your thin voice like water.
That damn moat
and all those things
swimming in it.

I tell you again,
it's part of the territory.
We agree my braids are too short.
There are rules to castles.
Water runs off me
into the moat.

You sigh, you'll call again
when you've figured it out.
Your voice glimmers, fades.
Morning star, are you there?
Hello? Are you there?

FOR MOTHER

She doesn't like my boots.
She laughs, says Where's your whip?
She means, Oh, you are not
what I expected.

We share the old joke. I'm trying,
Mother.
You are, you are, you're very trying.
When I visit, she smiles, watches me
come through the door, looks past me,
looks for the man.

I bring her books to read, lugging them
like burdens. They don't have happy endings.
She reads them like lessons,
she sees me, every woman in every book.
She worries about our dream,
the Prince who will kneel, will
lift my skirts, will find
my boots.

NEIGHBORS

Their bed collapses. Laughter
pushes through our common wall,
hers high and thin, his
a low huh-huh-huh, rhythmic
as bedsprings.

I am talking to a friend
on the telephone. They knock
on the wall, three short knocks.
It's like being rapped on the knuckles
by a nun. Do they think
I am talking to myself?

I move downstairs
at night with my books.
Their cuckoo clock keeps
me company, singing
the half-hour, the hour.

Like a circus act, the bed
collapses every night now.
I want to go there, tell them
Oh, please, come take my bed,
in ten years, it's never given out.

When they run a bath at 2 a.m.
I chew my lower lip.
Under one roof, we become
a family. I am
the maiden aunt.

GHOSTWRITTEN

Get it right! he says. Here, let me
help.
He will not touch her, yet he insists
on pushing her pen around.

He takes her pen into his mouth,
turning the possible words
on his tongue, tonguing the words
like marbles
or a breast.

We heard, or read
as told to someone, as told to
someone
that she would stand at his door
and thank him
and thank him and thank him.

LETTER FROM VERMONT

1.
Two days after love, after two showers,
four meals of barely acceptable vegetables,
three forbidden cigarettes — my last —
after endless cups of coffee too black
to swallow, still it is your taste,
your smell, that hangs in this green air.
Bitter as orange rind, or salty,
the salt of your shoulder against my mouth.
This does not rinse, nor
does it swallow.

2.
A man here tells the story
of tasting his first guava, at twelve.
Its juices send him back to his other first guava,
in Egypt, at four years old. He had forgotten.
Yes, I think, running my tongue
over my upper lip. Yes.
And this warmth rising from my palms
would buckle my knees if I stood.
Here, even the humidity sings, your voice
outside the shower,
outside my heart's eye.

3.

If this lasted a month, what would happen?
We would all go mad or, at the very least,
run out of paper. I need to come home,
you can bandage my head with your hands.
I want to pull off this acquired skin of words,
be only bones with you.

4.

This talking could make me crazy.
I remind myself daily I am here
voluntarily. Everyone in this room
loves more, reads more, bleeds more,
in more different places. I can't catch up.
The badge of membership is nerve ends
worn on the outside, a blue pencil,
bar sinister on a green background.
For all we know, the world has ended.
Someone says It's raining.
Or someone says
Why doesn't it rain?

TO THE STORYTELLER

for M. J.

One of your feet is on backwards.
Delicate, but nevertheless, there it is,
going the other way. Turnstiles
and escalators have always been impossible,
likewise, iceskating.
You say, Oh, don't mind me!

This constant coming and going, it cheers
travel agents, makes madmen out of doormen.
You try the going-off step, but what
is the audience to make of it?
Is this vaudeville?
Yes, but then again, no, you laugh,
dancing in crazy shoes,
making Italian goodbyes.

NO BALL GAME

In the stadium, lions always beckon
Come over here. Scratch our ears.

It seems they want
to explain, they want
to finish our sentences.
The crowd encourages
this tango, waving
with goblets,
with hot dogs.

Two steps forward, one back.

There are options.
We could spend time discussing
the ethics of absolution,
the lions' constant need
to be understood, the possibility
of detente between carnivores.

You and I and the rest of them
we huddle over here by the fence.
Someone shouts Go and we don't.
Someone else shouts Go and
we do.
We wonder, bone by bone,
if there's an easier way.

MY MOTHER DANCING WITH MY SON

She is teaching him to waltz. She bends
only slightly to his new height, he reaches
like new corn, rising and humming, all legs
and earnest rhythm.

Concentrating, breathing,
they count their way past me
and out the door:
two three four, two three four.

These bookends, they don't notice
the music ending.
These connections, they are dancing.

His teeth magically straighten.
She tells him he can be a surgeon,
a rock star. She tells him
good news sounds like this:
In Maine, more black flies this summer
because the water is purer. Irony,
she says, now you lead:
two three four, two three four.

ROSA'S CANTINA

When the crate arrives
in your front yard, its sides
fall away. There is a long, oaken bar,
scarred and dented,
encrusted with old silver dollars.

What a present!

Along the base, a rail for your boots,
spurs clicking on brass.
A mirror behind the bottles.
You look back at yourself,
check the angle of your hat,
the angle of your elbow,
tipping the whiskey back and down.

You turn, scan the room.
The piano begins, filling this place
with people. It seems
you should know them.

Consider.
There might be a card game.
You might be in it.
There might be a fight.
You might be in it.
You might stroll up the stairs,
turn down the hall,
knock on someone's door.

Nothing begins
until you begin it.

ISBN 0-914086-25-1

She will speak for us, hear us, know our secret trouble, our intimate imagery and behavior. She has the life-strength, curiosity, perception, language. To read her is to learn that we survive by caring for strangers. Willa Schneberg is a poet with healing power. I read her with gratitude.

Milton Kessler

This is the other side of the lullaby—equal parts reassurance and warning—the night world where the woman sleeps alone on old sheets, listening as the child listens, for the new and terrifying inflection of familiar sounds, foot-tap, pipe knock and something else: the enormous insistent music of her own waking, the aubade of her own voice.

Carol Muske

alicejamesbooks

a writers' cooperative with an emphasis on publishing poetry by women

138 Mount Auburn Street, Cambridge, Massachusetts 02138